ON LINES

By Chris Watt

Chris Watt is an author, screenwriter and film critic.

A graduate of the University of Northumbria, he is a regular contributor to *Flickfeast* and *Film Inquiry*, amongst others, and was the senior film critic for *Watch This Space Film Magazine*.

His first novel, *Peer Pressure*, was published in 2012. This is his first collection of poetry and shorter fiction.

He lives and works in Scotland.

@thechriswatt

First published in 2018

First Edition, First Printing (October 2018)

ISBN-9781723898716

Copyright © Chris Watt, 2018

Printed and bound by Kindle Direct Publishing

Introduction

One night, whilst on my twitter account, I decided to send a request out into the social media maelstrom.

I asked my followers to throw some suggestions at me, be it a word, a concept, a genre, whatever they liked, from which I would then write them a poem. The request went down surprisingly well, and many of my followers indulged me, throwing words like 'eccentricity', 'hope', 'vivacious', even 'analingus' (which I'm still not even sure is a real word), at me, while others would give me a concept, such as 'damp bath mat' and 'social media', to play with.

Within a month, I had written at least fifty poems, on a variety of random topics, words and emotions, all bound together by this most modern of communications. Given the source of my inspiration, the idea of ON LINES is to collect together all of my twitter poems into a volume of work that reflects both the experience of being alive in this contemporary, online world, but also the experience of stepping back from it, into a world of interaction, intimacy and love.

Therefore, the title of each poem, in this collection you hold in your hands, is the word, or concept that was given to me.

Art, as they say, is all about inspiration, and this collection represents this concept in the best possible sense. It would not exist without the many suggestions that were thrown at my twitter page, suggestions that came from people from many different backgrounds, ethnicities, countries and social spectrum.

Social media is made up of many pros and just as many, if not more, cons, and so I'm determined to shine a light on one of social media's more commendable traits: connection.

Poetry is all about connection, about allowing the reader to relive an emotion, or feel that they are not alone in an often harsh emotional spectrum. And if that isn't worth shouting about, in 280 characters or less, then perhaps I'm doing something wrong.

It wouldn't be the first time.

CW, @thechriswatt

For **Amy**

Part One: **Poetry**

Social Media

A blue tick for approval,
a green dot for connection.
Thumbs up from seven followers
heart emoji for affection.
Abbreviated language and a penchant
for debate.
A life online, a world gone blank,
a feast on empty plates.

Quintessence

Eyes met across a dance floor,
smiles and nods between the beers.
She takes a few steps forward,
and confirms the worst of fears.
Her auburn hair, her eyes pure blue.
A smile that overpowered.
I left the club as she approached.
Quintessence of a coward.

Empathy

I'm doing life for empathy,
No topic left unturned.
I fanned some flames,
but lit some too.
All injuries were earned.
A life lived out of focus,
and my back against the wall.
Pinned by expectations.
That is no life at all.

Damp Bath Mat

Damp bath mat on my bathroom floor.
The memory that you were here before.
Of tears and smiles, of truth and lies.
The pain remains, and then it dries.

Fleeting

The winds beat the glass panes,
the rains start again.
A storm loudly rages,
you whisper my name.
My hands trace your shape,
over white, silky skin.
My lips quiver, anxious,
for the kiss to begin.
The curtains are open,
the dusk lighting fades.
As shape turns to shadow,
my decisions are made.
I spoon close behind you,
you move to my touch,
I doubt my own instincts,
I love you too much.
My window frame rattles,
in time with my heart.
This memory will stick,
for tomorrow we'll part.

Roses

Pink Roses,
more than I can take.
Each petal falls,
for each mistake.

Near Miss

And in the end,
I turned away.
All confidence gone,
unsure what to say.
You lit up my mind,
you warmed up my heart.
But the first blush of love,
was never to start.

Transience

A glance that took me by surprise.
A meeting, first, between our eyes.
Fleeting, shyness takes its toll,
you look away, but maintain control.
This transience I can abide,
I'll live a lifetime with those eyes.

Felt

I felt you near,
like warm embrace.
A distance earned,
to touch your face.

Portraits

The earth spins on.
The sun still sets.
We met at noon, with no regrets.
Six years went by,
we made our plans.
Our lives entwined,
we took that chance.
But things grew stale,
dark shades of blue.
You looked away,
I hated you.
Portraits of loss,
from day to day.
Our time is up,
I walk away.

Lonely

I'm all alone in crowded rooms,
social gatherings and their kind.
But I'm more alone within the room,
that is my frame of mind.
I reach out, seeking kindness,
maybe friendship or just help.
They turn away, their cold neglect,
has never been more felt.
I'm searching not forgiveness,
or the trap of sympathy.
I want someone to save me,
from this fear of being me.

Hope

A wall built on a border,
a missile locked and set.
Ten children dead in crossfire,
our world lost on a bet.
Flickering news screen images,
that shake you to the core.
A lack of optimism on a broken, glass
strewn shore.
And yet I turn away to let that narrow
focus shift.
We all move forward,
one small step,
the world is set adrift.
Red banners scream out breaking news,
but focus elsewhere please.
It's only their assertiveness,
that brings us to our knees.
The planet spins, suns set, rains fall,
my fingers lock with yours.
Like laughter, love, the intimate,
hope knocks on many doors.

Time

If time is an illusion,
can someone wind it back?
I'm trapped in constant patterns,
they're causing me to crack.
My mind, it wanders often,
my work has left me cold.
My friends all seem together,
fortune favouring the bold.
I tail spin through my twenties,
chaos reigns, I try my best.
My folks say things get better.
I prepare to hold my breath.

Fridge

Hunger pangs at midnight,
as my legs fling to the floor.
Take careful steps, through shadow,
as I head towards a door.
Floorboards meet bare skin
and temperature is not so good.
Illumination from within,
a promise yet of food.
The fridge door swings aside
and I scratch my weary head.
These contents unfamiliar,
Should I go back to bed?
I squint through darkness,
now aware I don't know where I am.
A nights drinking taking its toll,
and I know I don't eat ham.
It's not my fridge, it's not my flat,
a masquerades at hand.
I need no more encouragement.
I'm done with one night stands.

Ice Cream

We took a walk on a summers day.
You told me there were things to say.
I bought a cone for us to share,
a scoop for each, to keep things fair.
You say you want to take a break,
I tell you it's a big mistake.
And then you spoke of how you felt,
my heart breaks as our ice cream melts.

Parenthood

The dawn patrol is on the move,
I hear feet pounding from my roof.
A voice screams "Daddy", I sit up,
she enters, bounces to my lap.
She doesn't know that I work late,
my emotions currently set to 'hate'.
A lack of sleep, of peace and rest,
a feeling, truly, to detest.
And then it happens, just like that,
my heart fills up, she starts to chat.
"I love you Daddy", makes sweet from
sour,
my day is made, despite the hour.

Eccentricity

A memory sticks, within my mind.
Though faded it may be.
I keep it close, as we were once.
I knew you, intimately.
The way you dressed to please yourself,
and how you managed looks,
from passers-by, a judgement glance.
They lived life by the book.
You never cared for rules or laws,
you set your standards higher.
You'd danced in public often,
and your passions burned like fire.
Your appetites exotic,
and your sexual tastes soft spoken.
You'd intimidate most suitors,
their attention gestures token.
They looked at you with puzzlement,
they looked, but did not see.
I looked and saw the beauty
of your eccentricity.

Crossroads

I stand at crossroads every day,
and dare to contemplate,
each person brushing by my side,
exclusive be their fates.
A story lies behind each glance,
a plot behind each meeting.
I feel the rush of life pass by,
a rush forever fleeting.
Each heart beats once,
as they pass by,
Emotions overthrown.
I breathe it in, eavesdropping on
a peek at lives unknown.
I wish for them a happy fate,
I wish for them no pain.
I take great comfort standing there.
I shall return again.

Next

From endless night,
you followed me,
a blaze of hope in tow.
I kept on walking,
through my life,
no sense of place to own.
At times I stopped,
disoriented,
face against the winds.
Waiting for that sun to rise,
and new day to begin.

Missing

The wind blew in my window.
Billowed curtains filled the air.
I missed you sitting next to me,
as more moments passed unshared.

Moon

I lay down on the grass,
and let my mind reflect my day.
A sea of stars before my eyes,
no clouds obscure my way.
My mind, it wanders, easily,
my eyes drink in this sight.
Infinite possibilities,
available each night.
It used to be experienced,
through secondary eyes.
We used to lie together,
my hand resting on your thigh.
We made our plans of years to come,
convinced we'd both be there.
But such plans shatter easily.
What good's a moon that isn't shared?

Greed

You took it all,
my life and breath,
you took my blood while warm.
And yet I stand defiant,
and hold firm against your storm.

Imagining

A blank page haunts my soul.
Of stories not yet told.
A pen in hand, I tremble.
To make that first assemble,
of people not yet breathing.
Emotions not worth leaving.
Imagining a better place.
One where I get to see her face.

Broken

I did not think to double back,
my life derailed and off the track.
Desires to be left alone,
I embrace the lonely in my home.

A patchwork quilt of jealousy.
The feeling overwhelms just me.
My passion dries up like a stream,
exposed to failures in my dreams.

I walked away, to life anew.
Too late to realise what to do.
Reflections changed, behind my back.
Surprise me like a heart attack.

I look for hope amongst despair.
I look to you but you're not there.
A shadow lifts, the memory gone.
The radio still plays our song.

We had it once and then it faded.
Left us broken, pained and jaded.
Memories are painted black.
The sun has set, I can't go back.

The path unclear, and yet, I walk.
We tried to change, we talked our talks.
These steps I take, towards the dawn,
are chess moves made. I take the pawn.

And rage sets in, amongst the tears.
Confirming all the worst of fears.
We had it all, we let it go.
A life reduced to grotesque show.

We never took the time to think,
to pull our life back from the brink.
I stepped away, but you stepped first.
The second step remained the worst.

Papers signed and promise broken,
all vows of love reduced to token.
And just like that, those years are gone.
Foundations worn from holding on.

Old habits and patterns return.
You struck the match, I felt the burn.
But wounds, like time, can heal and
mend.
I look to hope within the end.

The dawn has come, the path is clear.
A silhouette beyond my fear,
of something more, of deep surprise.
A smile, a face and loving eyes.

Bruise

These tears I shed for you
fall from my cheek and hit the floor.
I bore the pain of witness,
as I hid behind the door.
You scream his name in torment,
as he pulls tight at your hair.
He makes you strip before him.
You plead, he doesn't care.
His touch is rough, not tender,
as you sink down to your knees.
You pray for mercy and reprieve.
He hits you and you bleed.
Ten years go by, it haunts my mind,
dark clouds within my soul.
You left this world by hands of rage,
my youth he also stole.

Analingus

A thumping bass line rattles walls,
a blood red neon light.
My money clip near empty,
and I've been here half the night.

The girl is glistening with sweat,
she's on her seventh dance.
She smiles at me as she gyrates,
makes me think I have a chance.

She slides towards me, backwards now,
my cocaine grin's in rictus,
She peels her panties from her ass, and
begs for analingus.

She wants it now,
and I can tell,
It's not flirtatious lie.
My hand goes up, it starts at calf,
then makes its way to thigh.

And then to cheeks, so smooth, so soft,
I'm hard with expectation.
I lean into position as she starts her
masturbation.

But just as suddenly, she's gone,
the room is plunged to black.
My weak ass broadband let me down,
tech failure, tech attack.

The room is dark now, empty too,
as empty as my life.
I contemplate my options,
glance across to sleeping wife.

I ask myself, is she enough?
Does she know that I need more?
She's married more than she can take,
she's angel, not a whore.

Horror

A knock at my window,
and not at my door.
A knock at the window,
on the 23rd floor.

Touch

My head retracts,
as love descends.
I hide from fleeting, bitter ends.
Detached, I feel,
but feel too much.
The love had gone,
in spite of touch.

Conception

The crack of a fresh notebook,
opened newly, on my desk.
Pen point tapping at blank page.
Heart beating in my chest.
Perspiration at my brow,
I feel anticipation.
A sip of wine to open doors,
and speed up inspiration.
Then pen to paper, ink to air,
my ideas to fulfil.
My process like a snowball,
but I'm pushing it uphill.
The first word comes, the hardest part,
and this ones no exception.
The satisfaction hits me quick,
I'm high off sheer conception.

A.M.

The girl of my dreams,
in a literal sense.
A mirror of me,
that lacks the pretence.
I would wake from your arms,
from your wit and your grace,
were it not that I fear
the loss of your face.

Room

I'm alone in my grief,
in a room with no window.
There's a knock at my door,
but nobody's there.
That's the biggest knock of all.

Endings

I ask you not to cry so much,
a request that you defy.
And between extended silences,
you tell me I don't try.
Good words and bad words,
I find both are now exchanged.
I keep expressions limited,
it never hides the pain.
The story of our lives unfolds
as if I wasn't there.
The coldness and the cruelty,
don't mean I didn't care.
You leave me now, walk out that door,
and I'm left in despair.
Thinking only of good times
and the love we tried to share.

Lost

A dream I wake from, violently.
A dream drenched with despair.
Your name erased,
your face a myth,
a dream that you're not there.

All moments lost between us,
all those kisses, touches, looks.
Your shadow gone from sunlight's glare,
like pages torn from books.

The friends we share, deny your life,
and act as if you weren't.
It leaves me haunted by the sense
that our lives were not earned.

Your number gone, your email too,
the house you had was bare.
Our bed is empty, cold and stark.
No dream like this is fair.

I wake up dazed, my heartbeat pounds,
I reach out with my arm.
I feel you lying next to me.
No panic. No alarm.

I steady up and take my place,
beside you once again.
You gently move into my arms,
To ease my addled brain.

Regret

Gail sleeps in a cabin of regret.
Had a guy in the biblical sense,
now she's three men past the limit
and looking for a way out.
Takes a razor, takes twelve pills.
Six would do it, but she's killing for two.
No one here,
to settle her fears.

Mistaken

I feel your heartbeat,
against my ear.
I probably shouldn't
have used those shears.

Empty

He pats the seat and beckons,
for he's paid for the privilege.
He drinks in your body,
thirst to quench,
appetite to satiate.
You tremble.
He notices.
You hesitate.
He doesn't.
He makes his move,
you've none to make.
When will this stop?
What will it take?

Home

Two winds chill me.
North and South.
I stand, exposed and vulnerable
at the cliff edge of my choosing.

The waves beneath me crash to shore.
Debris of moisture taking flight.
It drenches me with salt,
salt that stings my open wounds.

A dash of sunlight finds its way
through cracks in the sky.
It warms my skin,
the briefest of reprieves.

The dark clouds continue,
rolling in to block the hope.
The way forward unclear
I turn towards my home.

The further I get away from you,
the closer you feel.
Your memory lodged.
Imprinted, indelible.

The longer I am kept from you,
the more I feel your pull.
Like ocean tide to shingle.
Crisp noises on the air.

Voices

A shadow thrown upon a wall.
A reflection in cracked glass.
A life fragmented and displaced.
A life lived in the past.
The mind is out of focus,
as you step outside your door.
Overwhelmed, you step back in.
Same feelings as before.
A circle has no end, it seems.
You're walking in one place.
You'll never know how common
is this feeling that you face.
The world spins forwards,
never back,
Take comfort in each dawn.
There's safety here in numbers,
realise you're not alone.

Stranger

I was followed home tonight.
I'm sure of it.
I can't be sure the gender.
But they were tall, imposing, silent.
I lock my door.
Dare not turn on the lights
for fear of attention drawn.
Naivety floods over me,
all gestures false tonight.
As I hear a key enter the lock.
She enters.
My partner.
My lover.
But I see nothing familiar.
No comfort.
Nothing.
She might as well have been the
stranger.

Cigarette

A cigarette haze,
on a warm, wet afternoon.
As I stare upon the pictures
which are hanging on my wall.
But a wall that can't be touched,
because there is no wall at all.

Shame

The rain hits my back.
Forty lashes for my troubles.
A cold baptism of shame.
A remorse from the sky.
My judgement day is here,
beneath clouds of my own making.

Ignorance

We met in a dream,
though it might have been Brighton.
We made love through the day,
then at night, put the light on.
We walked along beaches,
we walked along piers.
No signs yet of bitterness,
no signs yet of fears.
Two days spent together,
no regrets yet, no shame.
I'd cherish this memory,
but I've forgotten your name.

Jetlag

My plane flies from Brussels,
I head to Milan.
Layover in Austin,
then onto Japan.

I can't sleep in the air,
even worse on the ground,
for I can't hear your voice,
and I feel lost, not found.

It's always for business,
and it's never for leisure.
Two trayed plastic meals,
tend to dilute the pleasure.

The safety belt fastened.
My tray table tipped.
Another night elsewhere,
I feel ill equipped.

A crisp hotel mattress,
a fresh shower cap.
But I'm staring at ceilings,
not so much as a nap.

I need something other,
than comp'd B&B.
I crave you to be here,
to lie beside me.

The sky is before me,
I'm chasing the moon.
The stars fade to sunlight.
I'm heading home soon.

The days feel like months.
I am gripped by times power.
But I know you'll be with me,
though God knows at what hour.

Secrets

That empty, awkward feeling.
A remorse that sticks a pin into the past.
Emotion sets me reeling.
A betrayal of mind, that overwhelms me
fast.

Nowhere left to hide.
Each corner turned digs up a failure,
pure.
I can't stop the tide.
My image reduced to a mere caricature.

Part Two: **Flash Fiction & Miscellaneous**

Clive

Clive had spent all morning in the house and yet it wasn't until he had looked through every cupboard, smashing two glasses in the process and disturbing the dog, who, until this point, had been sleeping quietly in the corner, finally found the keys to the BMW parked outside, left the house, door wide open and got in the car, that he realised that he neither owned a car, nor lived in a house.

It was at this point that the police arrived.

First World Problems

They had been arguing for the better part of half an hour and a resolution was nowhere in sight. It had started, as these sort of arguments often do, over a trivial matter: What film to watch that night, before descending into a petty, vicious circle of offences, personal jibes, and very nearly the shaming of one side of the argument's virility.

His naturally.

It hadn't always been like this. The simpatico used to be kept in check by affection and an excitement that came from the thrill of the new. And yet, four years in, conversation and interaction had slowed to the point where both would only talk when something was needed, something fairly intangible and bland.

In other words, a perfect metaphor for the relationship.

Picking a restaurant, what music to play, which direction to go. Nothing sparked. Nothing excited or aroused. It was all about going through the motions.

And tonight, they had reached breaking point.

"I don't understand the question"

"I'll have to get back to you on that"

Response of that ilk was common that night. In the end, it was he who took the almost inevitable final step of finishing things.

He unplugged the phone and dumped it in the toilet in a drunken rage, thus ending his four year relationship with this particular model.

In retrospect, he may have over-reacted.

Boom Boom

I lost my virginity
in the nonfiction section
of my public library.
True story.

Love Is Blind

Discarded glasses
on my bedside table.
I never saw this coming.

Boom Boom Part Two

I cheated at my Rubik's Cube.
What chance did my Physics exam have?

Treatment

Once upon a time,
there was this bloke whose name I can't
remember.
Anyway, he had some problems,
overcame them
and lived happily ever after.

The End

Acknowledgements

The author would like to extend his gratitude to his followers on Twitter, without whom the majority of this book wouldn't exist.

Thanks and love also need to go to his family, his daughter Ellen, everyone at Flickfeast and Film Inquiry and his friends, particularly Linzie Gowans, Chris Whyte & Denise Papas Meechan.